TESTIMONIALS

My name is Glenn Morshower. I have been a professional actor for thirty-eight years, and have been blessed to work with many of the industry's best. I also travel extensively as a motivational speaker. My program, The Extra Mile, teaches people how to live a fully expressed life, by simply listening to, and obeying their inner whisper. This program has provided me with a sense of unparalleled satisfaction for many years.

When my friend and fellow speaker, Craig Duswalt, gave me Linda Fleischmann's book *How to Have a Stress Free Mortgage*, I felt better informed about what people need to do before they decide to buy. I became aware of so many things that I never knew were important, such as:

1. What credit scores really mean, and how they affect our interest rates.
2. Why we may want to think twice before co-signing a relative's car, or home loan.

Linda is the front runner in her field. She has broken down the components of the mortgage process from beginning to end in a simple and understandable way.

I highly recommend that anyone thinking about buying a home, or needing to refinance their existing home, read *How to Have a Stress Free Mortgage*. If you want to have that stress free experience that few people are able to have when getting a home loan, be sure to read Linda Fleischmann's book first.

-**Glenn Morshower**, Professional Actor

A large part of the Broughton Hotels success and acquisition model is studying new markets, evaluating individual properties, assessing their potential worth, and determining if the acquisition will add value to our growing portfolio. This same principle applies to the aspiring homeowner. Understanding how to get a mortgage loan and then actually securing one in today's complicated market is complicated and stressful. Linda's book, *How to Have a Stress Free Mortgage*, is the ideal GPS device to navigate the mine fields associated with the home mortgage and lending process. Linda's easy to understand, step-by-step book (I call it a "battle plan") moves the dream of home ownership from fantasy to reality."

-**Larry Broughton**, Founder & CEO,
broughtonHOTELS.com, BROUGHTONadvisory.com,
NaVOBA's Entrepreneur of the Year, Ernst & Young's
Entrepreneur of the Year, Former Special Forces Operator
(the Green Berets).

HOW TO HAVE A STRESS FREE MORTGAGE

HOW TO HAVE A
STRESS
FREE
MORTGAGE

Insider Tips
From a Certified Mortgage Broker to Help Save You
Time, Money, and Frustration

LINDA FLEISCHMANN
www.stressfreemortgage.com

NEW YORK

How to Have a Stress Free Mortgage

Insider Tips From a Certified Mortgage Broker to Help Save You
Time, Money, and Frustration

Printed in the United States of America
Fleischmann, Linda
How to Have a Stress Free Mortgage, by Linda Fleischmann

ISBN   9781614482680 (paperback)
ISBN   9781614482697 (eBook)
Library of Congress Control Number: 2 012935390

To order, please call 661-295-0555 or

www.stressfreemortgage.com

Email inquiries to linda@stressfreemortgage.com

Cover design by Dawn Teagarden

Photos by R&R Photography

Disclaimer: The purpose of this book is to educate and provide general information
regarding mortgages and loans. The author or publisher does not guarantee that
anyone following these suggestions or guidelines will have a stress free mortgage
experience. The author or publisher shall have neither liability nor responsibility to
anyone with respect to any loss or damage caused, or alleged to be caused, directly
or indirectly by the information contained in this book.

Morgan James Publishing
The Entrepreneurial Publisher
5 Penn Plaza, 23rd Floor, New York City, New York 10001
(212) 655-5470 office • (516) 908-4496 fax
www.MorganJamesPublishing.com

In an effort to support local communities, raise awareness and funds, Morgan James Publishing
donates a percentage of all book sales for the life of each book to Habitat for Humanity Peninsula
and Greater Williamsburg.

Get involved today, visit
www.MorganJamesBuilds.com.

Habitat
for Humanity®
Peninsula and
Greater Williamsburg
Building Partner

To Mark, my love and partner in life.
Without you, I would never have accomplished all that I have done.
Thanks for always supporting me and giving me advice that in the
end is always the right choice. You are my inspiration, and you make
me a better person. Together, anything is possible.

To Lexie and Michael. You are both my joy in life.
You are wonderful kids and turning into amazing adults and I am so
proud of both of you.

To my dad who always supported me and believed in me...
I know that you are watching over me now and smiling.

To my mom who doesn't always understand me or my life
and what I do, but who is always there to listen.

To my realtors that help me work with our buyers and realize their
dreams, you are all special.

To all the clients that I have helped in the past and all the
clients in the future, this is for you.

ABOUT THE AUTHOR

Linda Fleischmann started in the mortgage industry in 1999 when she opened a mortgage company in Southern California. Linda has helped thousands of clients both purchase their homes and refinance their home loans.

Linda's journey in the banking industry began in 1985 when she was employed as a part time bank teller by California Federal Bank. In 1992, she was promoted to Branch Manager, a position she held until she left the company in 1998. Learning the ins and outs of the mortgage business at WMC Mortgage, formerly Weyerhaeuser Mortgage, Linda then opened Loan Connectors, a company whose excellent reputation was supported by its referral based client list. In 2011, Linda closed Loan Connectors in order to open Stress Free Mortgage and focus on her clients and educating the public about the mortgage industry.

No one is more passionate about loans than Linda Fleischmann. She will do whatever it takes to achieve customer satisfaction even if it means telling someone NOT to do a loan. Her honesty and knowledge of the loan and mortgage business has led her to maintain success even during trying economic times. She is an active member of various prestigious organizations in her hometown of Santa Clarita, California, including the Santa Clarita Chamber of Commerce, Women Entrepreneurs of the Santa Clarita Valley, and Valencia Business Associates. She is a Certified Mortgage Consultant with the National Association of Mortgage Brokers, and is also affiliated with the California Association of Mortgage Professionals. Linda has spoken on numerous radio stations and has given seminars for first time buyers.

Linda and her husband Mark live in Southern California with their two children, Lexie and Michael and their dog, Sadie.

CONTENTS

INTRODUCTION

Idecided to write *How to Have a Stress Free Mortgage* when I realized that people were in trouble. With so many rules and regulations, misinformation and misrepresentation, many clients were forced into situations that were not in their best interest. This book can help make the process of getting a mortgage much easier.

Buying a home should be an exciting process that is supported by a team of players to help you. It is an industry that is based on trust since most of the "team" may know more than you do. With all the knowledge I have accumulated over the years, I realized that more people needed to benefit from this wealth of information so that they too, could make the best choices.

Thousands of clients have been successful in obtaining loans for their new homes with the information in this book. I have heard the comment, "That was so simple," more than a few times. My job is to make the process of securing a mortgage in a simple manner so that you can enjoy the rollercoaster as much as possible.

Most people don't understand the requirements necessary for obtaining a loan. With this book as a guide, you will be armed with information that will help you become more knowledgeable and confident when you approach your next mortgage. Whether you are a first time buyer, repeat buyer or in the process of refinancing, this book will offer information and insights that can open the way for you to make wise decisions.

Always consult your loan officer and your tax advisor with the specifics of your situation, however, even as guidelines and regulations change in the mortgage industry, *How to Have a Stress Free Mortgage* can always be used as a guide.

Linda Fleischmann

How to Have a Stress-Free Mortgage: Insider Tips from a Certified Mortgage Broker to Help Save you Time, Money, and Frustration

1

My Story

I am passionate about writing a book about mortgages, because I love what I do. I have been in the financial industry for nearly twenty-five years, but I was not always involved in just the mortgage business. Although I thought loans were fascinating, I was on the sidelines for the first half of my career. You may be asking, why am I qualified to give advice, and why did I write this book? Here is my story.

I began my thirteen year career at a bank, as a part-time teller while going to college. Starting at the bottom, I kept moving up the ladder, and seven years later I became a branch manager. Throughout this time, one of the bank's main goals was to expand its lending operations. As the branch manager, I was responsible for both consumer lending, such as car loans, home equity loans, and residential lending or mortgages, and I learned a lot about this area. I was personally responsible for home equity loans and lines of credit. By doing this, I had to master the bank policy concerning lending guidelines, which included calculating debt ratios. The corporate office, however, was responsible for approving and finalizing the loan.

Eventually, the bank where I worked went through a merger. It was brutal, but I stayed with it and held my position at the top of the company. However, a few years later when the bank began another merger, I decided it was time to start looking for another job.

At that point, I had been in banking since college and was in the thirteenth year of my career in the field. But, I still wasn't sure about what I wanted to do. I had an opportunity to get into mortgage loans by starting a retail branch for a mortgage company. My job was to get the loans that other banks might decline, because the mortgage company I joined was in the "subprime" business. That was the first time I ever heard the word subprime. Subprime means, that the company closed loans for people who had poor credit or couldn't prove their income. While I was certainly up for the challenge, I really did not have the extensive knowledge I needed about the mortgage industry. My early days in this field represented a trial by fire. I still refer to this part of my training as "figure it out as you go!"

I started my job with the mortgage company at a time when the subprime industry was going through its first set of trials and tribulations. Indeed, right when I started in August, 1998, the company started closing down departments right and left. When the call center closed along with other departments, the floor of the building where I worked kept getting less and less crowded.

Finally, after only three and a half months of learning the subprime mortgage lending business, I had a terrible shock.

Imagine this scenario: During Thanksgiving week, the company had been closed on Thursday and Friday. However, as I drove into the garage on my way to work on Monday morning, my parking pass wouldn't let me enter. At first I was not overly concerned about this as I could get in by using the manual override button. From there, I proceeded into the parking garage office to ask why my card was not working. The attendant couldn't find my information on the computer, so he walked over to a wire rack and began looking through a bunch of papers. As he continued rifling through the stack, I began to get more and more nervous. I remembered seeing so many people laid off in the past months. I began to hope this was just a misunderstanding about parking arrangements. But, sure enough, the man came back with a piece of a paper and said, "Linda Fleischmann?" After I responded, he said flatly, "This says you've been terminated."

"WHAT? Seriously? This is how I find out that I've been laid off?"

Wow, I thought that sort of thing only happened in the movies. I went straight in to talk to my boss. He also told me flatly that, yes, the company had laid off my entire department, and quite frankly, he was not very nice about it. Apparently, this sort of incident was par for the course in the mortgage industry at the time. When I went to deliver the news in person to my staff members, who were all still working, they had no idea what had just happened. After that, we all packed up and left for good.

Well, what can I say? I wasn't completely surprised, except for the ridiculous way I found out about the layoff.

So, there I was, completely out of a job for the first time since I was sixteen years old. After spending some time trying to figure out what I wanted to do, I came to the realization that I really do love arranging loans! More importantly, I figured out that I could do this business on my own by opening my own mortgage company. So, I talked with my assistant who had come with me from the bank to the mortgage company and who was also out of work, and we started a brand new mortgage company.

Although we began working in a small office in my home, we moved into a 700 square-foot office space after only one month. About a year later, we moved into another office with double the space. When I started my company, I focused on a few philosophies that I felt were critical for any business. The most important being, we take care of the customers, just as I had always done as a branch manager, making sure they always got the best deal. I also made sure clients understood the loans they were getting and that when they went into escrow, they would never be surprised by the closing statements. In particular, we ensured that our clients would always know in advance their loan terms, costs and fees, and I would communicate with them throughout the loan process. Quite honestly, I didn't know any other way to do business. Our slogan was "Loans Made Simple," because these were, and still are, the main goals of our company. We focus on making even the most complicated financial transaction as simple for the client as possible.

Like any other business, there was a lot to learn. Indeed, each loan is a learning experience in itself! Believe me when I tell you that I have learned a lot in the eleven years that I have been closing loans. One thing about the mortgage industry that is different from any other profession is that no two loans are ever completely the same. Each client has his or her unique experiences and stories. Also, each lender has its own individual guidelines. Finally, every mortgage loan I handle is very different from the previous one. There is no template, just experience. Even today, I still come upon unique scenarios. For me, that has been the interesting part about this business. I like the challenge that this industry brings in solving the problems that invariably arise in the course of working on every loan. Problem solving is an integral part of the process. If I do my job correctly, most of the time a client will not even know that there was a problem, unless of course, it stops the loan from closing. But, I figure out how to work out most of the problems that arise along the way, and that's what I love most about my work.

FIGURING IT OUT AND CLOSING LOANS

One thing that sets me apart from other mortgage brokers is that I can tell fairly early on when a problem is insurmountable, and the loan won't happen. In these cases, I do not let the process drag on until the frustration level for all parties goes beyond comprehension. I do not let my clients put a lot of time and energy into securing a loan only to have it not close. For this reason, I am very upfront about the client's ability to qualify for a mortgage. This is one the core values of my business. I do the right thing for my clients and realtors, so that we can all achieve the main objective, which is to close the purchase transaction and have the client moving into a new home. In the case of a refinance, it is the same objective. You don't waste a client's time on a loan that will not close.

One time, I had some clients who just didn't believe I could get them a loan. They had some credit and income challenges. Nevertheless, I assured them that their loan would be approved, and they would be moving into the new home they wanted. They went along thinking they were "humoring" me, but kept telling me that they didn't believe it would truly work. A week before they went to closing, I asked the clients whether they had given their landlord notice, since they would be closing that week, and they hadn't. The client said, "Linda, I still don't believe it's really going to close!" They moved into their new home that same week.

Being in the mortgage business gives me the opportunity to do so many things that I love. I love working with people, interacting with them, hearing their stories, and being able to figure out the best way to help them. I love being able to help get people new homes or better loans for homes they already own. The most difficult part of my job is the frustration of knowing that if I had had the opportunity to talk with many of my clients a few months or years before they were going to purchase a house, I could have made the process much easier and better for them. Many people who currently are not able to secure the financing they need would have been able to get a loan and buy the home of their dreams. Unfortunately, by the time some of these people come to me to help them get a loan, it's too late. The damage has already been done. That's why I wrote this book that will help people understand the pitfalls, many of which they would never think of on their own or consider in their quest to own a home.

Having said that, it is important to bear in mind that the mortgage industry is in a constant state of flux and guidelines change constantly. Indeed, even as I am writing this book, many loan qualification criteria and processes are changing. Against that background, this book should be seen as only a guide. However, it walks readers through many things they can do to be in the best position to buy. I know that if I can give you one tip or piece of advice you didn't know before and that helps you get through either buying a new home or refinancing your existing loan, I will have accomplished what I set out to do. Namely, making your home loan process simple and alleviate the frustration, time and money spent on getting a home loan.

Use a FREE QR Reader App on your SmartPhone to scan and enjoy!

 Scan here for some testimonials from clients that have enjoyed a Stress Free Mortgage!

2

Before Deciding to Take the Big Step

Kelly was referred to me by a realtor because she wanted to buy a home. She was a single mother who felt she could never afford one. Although she had saved a small amount of money, she believed she would have to make a 20% down payment in order to purchase. When she called me, I found that Kelly had immaculate credit, a solid job, and the price of the house she wanted fit right into her budget. She had planned ahead without even realizing it by paying her bills on time and saving money. Even after we spoke and I told her that she could buy what she wanted, she didn't believe me right up until she and her realtor put in an offer that was accepted, and she was in escrow!

You are probably sitting at home right now thinking about how nice it would be to buy a house. You've been living with your parents or in an apartment, or you have been renting, wondering where your money is going every time you write the check.

We all know where it goes. It goes to the landlord who owns the property because they made the decision to buy real estate a long time ago.

So, now it's your turn. What do you do? Are you able to buy? How much cash will you need? What will it cost? Are you ready? Let's talk about the things that you will need to consider before you start the loan process to make it as smooth as possible.

INCOME

Lenders want to know that you've had a job for the past two years and that you've made steady income. If you've been in the same job for the past two years, that's a great start. If you've changed jobs, but are still in the same industry or doing the same type of job, that's okay too.

Changing jobs frequently, however, can suggest to lenders that you are not particularly stable. Therefore, it is important to try to maintain a steady history in the job market. If you are working on an hourly basis, but you have overtime, be aware that lenders will not be able to use your overtime income to qualify you for a loan unless you can show a history of receiving that same overtime income for at least two years. The same thing applies to income from bonuses, commissions and having additional employment, such as a second job. Even though you know you are making more money, which is a great thing, you may not be able to qualify for as large a loan as you can really afford because you can use only your hourly wage or base salary.

If you are in the sales industry, be aware that unless you've been in sales for two years and can demonstrate the commissions you earn monthly, lenders will not likely take into account the commission income. Unless you have a very steady history of commission income to look at, lenders won't use what you are presently making.

Now, let's assume that you have been working for someone else and you decide to go out on your own and join the world of self-employed business owners. This is what I would call the Kiss of Death! You need to be self-employed for at least two years (there's that two year rule again) before you can successfully apply for a mortgage loan. There are exceptions to this rule, but they are few and far between. So, if you're thinking about leaving your nice salaried job to become self-employed and you want to buy a new house, your best option is to buy the house first, and then go out on your own. At the same time however, you cannot be sure what your income will be once you become self-employed. Therefore, it might behoove you to wait the two years to make sure you will be able to afford the house before considering a loan. No one wants you to get in over your head by buying a house at the wrong time.

This is why long-term planning is important.

I often tell my clients that eating macaroni and cheese every night to make a mortgage payment is no way to live! No matter what mortgage you might be able to qualify for now, it is important to take into account the amount you will have to pay later. If you could possibly have a problem making the mortgage, reconsider now!

The other thing to think about is changing professions. If you are a welder and decide to get out of the heat and out on the road by becoming a truck driver, lenders will want to see you driving for two years before giving you a loan. In other words, lenders are looking for a track record in both the profession and the position. There should at least be similarities that tie your work history together. For example, if your old job was as a secretary and you are now an executive assistant, that would work as a track record of being in the same profession. However, if you decide to become a teacher, lenders will be looking for you to have the two-year work history or the education to become a teacher.

Speaking of education, if you are just graduating from college or a vocational school and have a degree, you would not have to have two years of work experience before qualifying for a mortgage loan. As long as you have a degree or diploma from the school, many lenders will overlook the two-year rule related to job history.

SELF-EMPLOYED AND OTHERS WITH DEDUCTIONS

In this section I want to highlight a special dilemma that affects the self-employed when it comes to the lender or mortgage underwriter. The processes related to income tax and mortgage loans can be at odds with each other, so it is important to know what pitfalls to avoid. Each year, you probably visit an accountant to prepare your tax return. Or, if you are really brave, you may do this yourself. In preparing tax returns, the goal is usually to pay as little tax as possible. Therefore, you take the gross income from your business and subtract all the business expenses you possibly can. These expenses can range from the costs related to your car or truck, business meals and entertainment, or travel. Let's say your gross income was $150,000 for the year, but you can subtract expenses of $110,000. Thus, you would pay taxes on your actual income, which is now $40,000. This is also the amount that will be used to qualify you for a mortgage loan. Whether that is your true income or not, whatever you declare to the IRS is your income, and it will be used to qualify you for a loan. Therefore, in the period before you buy a house, you may have to make decisions about whether you are going to pay more tax and write off fewer expenses or raise your income to qualify for the home you want to buy. You really have to consider these issues years in advance, since mortgage lenders and underwriters will be looking at the past two years of income on your tax returns. Keep in mind that you should always consult with your tax preparer or CPA for the tax rules as I am not giving tax advice, but simply providing some insight on what an underwriter will be looking at in approving your loan.

SALARIED WITH BENEFITS

This consideration may apply even if you are not self-employed but are in a profession that allows you to write off expenses for which your employer does not reimburse you. Let me give you some examples. I have many clients in the entertainment industry who receive regular paychecks and W-2s for the work they do throughout the year. However, many of them travel, some take clients out to lunch or dinner, and some, such as make-up artists, have to buy their own products. I also have clients who are police officers, firemen, or sheriffs. Even though they are salaried employees, they can write off their uniforms, travel, and so forth. Although people in this category do not file as self employed, their business expenses have a huge impact on their incomes. These employee business expenses, which are reported on Form 2106 on your tax return, are deducted directly off of the total income earned for tax purposes. They are also deducted for the purposes of securing a mortgage loan.

For example, one of my clients who is a make-up artist had W-2 income of $40,000 a year. This income would have been enough to qualify her for the house she wanted to purchase. However, she had 2106 expenses that totaled $20,000! That meant that her income for underwriting purposes was only $20,000, not nearly enough to qualify to buy the house she wanted. Therefore, when you are meeting with your tax preparer, or if you are doing your taxes yourself, it is important to keep the impact of business expenses in mind so that you will also be prepared when the time comes to purchase or refinance your home.

Similarly, if you are a salaried or W-2 employee and have a side business, own other real estate, or have a partnership, it is critical to let your loan officer know this up front. As part of the loan approval process, the lender will file an IRS form, called a 4506T, to get a snapshot of your tax return and verify the income and documentation you provided. They do this to make sure that the application you submit for a loan matches the documentation you filed with the government. I had a client who sold a painting and after all of his expenses were deducted; he had a loss of $5,000. This amount was deducted from his income for tax purposes. Having a business like this can provide a nice tax write off, but it will also affect how much you can qualify for when you want to finance a house. Letting your loan officer know about these circumstances up front can help them put your loan together correctly and ensure there is no information missing, and no surprises later.

CO-SIGNING LOANS

Some people are simply kind and generous. Because of this, they agree to co-sign on credit for their relatives, boyfriends, best friends, or even not-so-great friends they can't say "No" to. If you are thinking of co-signing a loan, it is critical to keep in mind that their debt will become your debt. Regardless of who may be making the payments, how they make them will be critical to you. I will be talking later about credit, so I'm not going to talk about how late payments may affect you here. But, I want to make sure you understand how debts you co-sign for others can affect your ability to finance a house. In particular, you must consider that no matter who pays it, it is your debt in the eyes of a mortgage underwriter.

If the person for whom you co-signed a loan is making the payments directly to the creditor, you will need to show canceled checks for 12 months to demonstrate that you do not have to include that payment with your monthly debt payments. If they are paying you cash, and you are making the payments, then the debt payments are yours. If I had to pick the best way to take care of a car lease or other payments made under a co-signing arrangement, it would be to have the person involved write a monthly check to the creditor but give it to you. Then, you mail the payment to the creditor. This method addresses two critical issues. First, you know the payment is being made on time every month. Second, you are not writing out the payment from your account, and you will be able to show the canceled checks to demonstrate to a potential lender that the payments are not coming out of your account each month. This also helps to preserve your relationships. I have seen relationships between family members and close friends disintegrate when a person applies for a loan and learns that their brother, who swore to make that car payment diligently every month, didn't do it for whatever reason. If that happens, your credit will be toast. Also, if you are not actually co-signing, but you are buying for the other person, then even if you have the cancelled checks showing someone else is making the payments, it is still your debt because you are the only person on the loan.

Speaking of car loans—since these are the most common things people co-sign—it may be helpful to note that lenders will not hold them against you if you have less than 10 months left to make payments, and you are applying for a conventional loan. However, if you are getting an FHA loan, car payments do count as part of your total debt until the debt is fully paid off. Also, if your car is leased, the payments will still be added to your debt. The underwriter will assume that your payments will continue into the future as you will likely get another car when you turn in the one currently under lease.

DIVORCE

How does divorce affect your ability to buy or refinance? There are a few issues you should consider. First, if you have a legal document from the court stating that you and your former spouse have agreed on the division of assets and who is paying what bills, it should be okay to apply for a mortgage loan. You should ensure that each spouse is making the payments they are responsible for from separate bank accounts so that the financial aspects of the relationship are clear and completely separate. If you have a home that you and your former spouse purchased together, you will need to have a legal document showing which spouse is making the payments. Otherwise, you may have a problem, especially if the divorce is not final. If you are legally separated and the legal separation papers spell out who is paying for what, that document can be shown to an underwriter to show who is responsible for which debt. However, if you decide to separate from your spouse and you have done all the paperwork yourself or have agreed only verbally on who will pay which bills, all the debts will be treated as joint obligations, and you will be held responsible for the total debt when applying for a loan.

When your divorce is final and the divorce decree states that one spouse gets the house and pays the mortgage, that document itself does not change the mortgage note for the loan. For example, if one spouse signs a quitclaim deed giving up his or her rights to the property, that does not take his or her name off the loan itself. That means you will be responsible for the mortgage on the property. For this reason, I strongly advise the spouse who plans to keep the property to refinance the mortgage into their name alone as soon as possible. This is the only way the other spouse's name can come off the mortgage loan.

Applying for a mortgage can be stressful, but if you use the pointers I've described above, it can help you navigate through the murky waters, and I promise you will encounter much less stress when you apply for a mortgage loan.

3

Credit Dos and Don'ts

Iasked my client, Janet, as we were discussing her being able to purchase a home, what her credit was like. Does she pay her bills on time? Does she have any late payments, collections, or bankruptcies? She responded that she thought it was okay. As far as she knew, her credit should be good. So, after Janet left and I put her loan together, I pulled her credit report. I waited eagerly for the over 700 credit score that I knew she would have based on our conversation earlier. As her credit report came up on my computer and I saw her credit score, I was struck by that familiar pang, "Does she really not know, or is she in denial?" Janet's score was 579. She had many collection accounts and late payments. Her ability to get a good loan, or a loan at all, was all but done. I wished I could have given her advice years ago, so that she could buy her home today. As it was, I was faced with giving her the news that she would need to fix her credit and come back to buy a house in a year or so.

Here's what everyone should know about credit scores long before considering a home purchase.

CREDIT AND FICO SCORES

Over the past ten years, I have talked to more than 5,000 clients, and one of the first questions I always ask is about their credit. I get a variety of answers, ranging from "Excellent!" to "Not so good" to "I have no idea!" Unfortunately, with the credit scoring system we have, most people seeking credit for a loan really don't know how their credit is unless it is REALLY good or REALLY bad, and who could blame them?

The FICO system is inconsistent and many times inaccurate. It has changed over the years. Let's take a look at credit, how it works, how you are scored, and some of the issues surrounding it.

New Century Mortgage went out of business in February of 2007 and that was the day that subprime lending, which was a huge piece of the lending world, died. New Century Mortgage was a major player and one of the top three companies originating subprime loans when it closed its doors forever. Although much has been written about subprime lending and the majority of it has not been positive, it did have its place. When subprime mortgages were put together in the right way for the right clients, they were beneficial for all parties concerned.

In today's market, the range of credit scores is the same, but they mean something completely different. Here's a look at what the differences are from the period before the market collapsed and now:

CREDIT SCORE BEFORE 2008	CREDIT SCORE AFTER 2008	GRADE	WHAT THIS MEANS TO YOU
720+	740+	A++	Golden credit, can get any loan available
680-719	720-739	A	Really good, but not perfect
640-679	700-719	B	Good, but some blemishes.
620-639	680-699	C	Not good, but can find a decent loan
580-619	640-679	D	Bad credit, but can still get you a loan with higher rates and fees
550-579	620-639	D-	Just barely able to finance
500-549	619 and below	F	You need to pay your bills!!! No conventional loan for you!

Clearly, a few years ago a score of 720 or above qualified for the best rates and loan terms a borrower could get. Today, that is not the case. To be rated with having the best credit, a borrower needs to have a FICO score of over 740. Otherwise, the loan will most likely cost them money or possibly create a higher interest rate. Although a person's credit score combines with other factors in determining eligibility for borrowing, any score below 740 is no longer considered great credit. If you have a FICO score below 620, it means that it will be a challenge to get a loan. Although there are a few lenders that may still extend financing, there will be both a higher rate and cost.

A borrower would be better off raising their credit score to bring it over 620 before applying for a mortgage than paying the higher cost or down payment to get a loan. In the long run, there are definite benefits to having a higher credit score.

Now, I know you must be asking, "What makes up my credit score and how does this whole thing work?" I will tell you that in my thirteen plus years of experience in mortgage lending, I have found that credit is not always fair, correct, or valid. However, that is the system we have to live with, and the best defense is to have as much information as possible in order to work within the system and make it work for you. Let's look at some of the items that affect credit scores.

We all know, or should know, that if you don't make payments on the items that you've charged, that's a bad thing! If your payment was due on March 15, and you didn't pay it until March 20 and had a late charge assessed by the credit card company, this is not considered as a late payment on your credit report. However, if the credit company didn't receive your payment until after April 15 and reported the account to the credit bureaus as 30 days late, this does go on your credit report. The reporting gets worse over time. If you still haven't paid that credit card by May 15, the company will report that you had a 60-day late payment and so on. The longer it takes for you to make that payment (30, 60, 90, or 120+ days), the more it will lower your credit score.

Now, if you never pay the bill, then it becomes either a charge-off, which means that the credit card company wrote your debt off, or a collection, which means that they sold it to a collection agency to have them try and collect from you. These measures have a huge impact on your credit score.

Of course there are special circumstances that arise even if you are always diligent about paying your bills each month. Let's say, for example, that you always make your payments on time and have never been late. But, you made a visit to the doctor and you have insurance to pay for that visit. Suddenly, six months later, you find out that not only did the insurance company not pay the doctor, but also no one contacted you to tell you that you had to pay that bill. Now, the doctor's office has sent that bill to a collection agency, and they are harassing you to get the money! Your perfect credit score just dropped from 750 to 680, because of that one collection on your unblemished credit history. Now, these are not exact numbers; I am just giving you a good idea of what can happen.

Public records have the heaviest weight on your credit score, and they include bankruptcy, judgments, and tax liens. Once you have them, they do not come off your credit report for ten years. Therefore, you should think carefully before deciding not to pay what you owe.

Getting new credit also has an impact on your FICO scores, and accepting those solicitations for credit you receive in the mail may be lowering your credit score. When you say "Yes" to those offers, you are getting both a new inquiry on your credit report and a brand new credit card, both of which can lower your score.

With respect to mortgage inquiries, you can have many inquiries on your credit within a twelve day period, and it will count as only one inquiry. I suppose the assumption is that if you apply for ten credit cards, you could actually get ten credit cards. But, even though there may be many inquiries for a mortgage, you will not be purchasing five or ten houses at once! However, I wouldn't test this theory too vigorously. I once had a client who didn't believe, or like, the amount I told him he was qualified to borrow. He decided to shop for mortgages among more than twenty lenders and brokers. All he succeeded in doing was lowering his credit score by more than 50 points!

REVOLVING CREDIT

In today's market, credit card companies have begun to lower the amount of available credit on credit cards. Maybe you've had several credit cards and you have different limits on each of them. Let's say, for example, that you have a Visa card with a $20,000 limit, and you owe $5,000 on it. You have another Visa card with a $5,000 limit and a balance of $2,000, and a Sears card with a $500 limit and a balance of $400. Thus, all your limits together total $25,500, and the balances total $7,400. That is an overall percentage of 29%. The optimum percentage is 30%. However, even though all together your percentage of utilized credit is close to the optimum, your Sears card is at 80% of its limit. This alone will make your credit score drop significantly. This is true, even if you pay everything on time and have never had any bad credit, ever!! So, now you say, "Okay, let me pay off this small Sears card. I'm good, right?" The answer is yes, if everything else stays the same. But, here's what's happening today. Credit card companies are cutting back on the limits that people have been enjoying for the past twenty years. So, you can pay off your Sears card and get a notice in the mail from one Visa card that the $20,000 limit you've had for the past fifteen years has been lowered to $7,000. You are now at 70% of your limit, and your credit score just dropped significantly without you lifting a finger!

MYTHS AND FACTS ABOUT CREDIT

I have heard since I started in this business that too much credit can hurt you, so close out your credit cards and keep only one or two. That is not true! It is all about the proportion of balances you keep on each card. If you already have enough credit cards, then you don't need more, and getting new credit can hurt your credit scores. Keeping your oldest credit cards open is critical as they have the longest history. If you have been paying them on time, they are reporting good payment histories to the credit bureaus. The longer your payment history, the better your scores will be. If you've just started with getting credit, then you need to build up a good credit history. Getting credit cards, making some purchases, and then paying them off or down every month is an excellent way to build credit. If you feel like you have too many credit cards, you should close out the one you opened most recently rather than just picking any card. Choose wisely as your credit scores depend on it!

Another thing to consider is balance transfers. When you get that offer in the mail saying that you can make a balance transfer from one credit card to another and have a zero percent interest rate, whether or not you should do it totally depends on your answer to the following question: ARE YOU PLANNING TO BUY OR REFINANCE IN THE NEXT SIX MONTHS? If you are, then a balance transfer will not work in your favor, because you will most likely have a higher proportion of debt to your credit limit, and this will lower your scores. If you are not planning to buy or refinance, making the balance transfer makes sense as it will save you money in interest to the credit card companies.

FORECLOSURE, BANKRUPTCY AND SHORT SALES

Here's an issue that is becoming even more prevalent in the period since 2008. Over recent months, I have seen thousands of credit reports and there have been a fair share of bankruptcy filings that show up. There have also been many foreclosures and short sales. Foreclosure filings were reported on more than 2.3 million properties, or 1 in 54 homes, in 2008. That's an 81% increase from 2007 and a 225% increase from 2006, according to the foreclosure data firm RealtyTrac. What that means is that more people than ever will have a foreclosure on their credit report, and they need to know how that will impact their ability to buy a house in the future. A bankruptcy stops you from buying a home for a minimum of two years if you are applying for an FHA loan AND you had extenuating circumstances. These may include medical issues or a job loss. The simple explanation, "I had too much debt and couldn't pay it all" does not cut it.

For conventional loans, it will be four years before you can purchase again and then there will be more restrictions on what your credit score can be. A short sale also shows on your credit report as "settled for less than balance owed." In most cases, the lender considers a short sale the same as a foreclosure, although if you were never late on your mortgage payments, there are circumstances where you may be able to buy soon after a short sale. If you did have a short sale with and had late mortgage payments, then as of today, FHA will allow you to buy again after 3 years. This may change again, as guidelines regarding credit are ever changing. Please check with your loan officer on the guidelines before you consider a short sale or foreclosure. After a Bankruptcy, many people are scared to have any credit in case they repeat the mistakes of the past. If you ever plan on buying a home, you need to reestablish credit to show the lender that you can handle making payments. Late payments to creditors after a bankruptcy is also an issue, so be very careful to make all of the payments on time.

OLD VS. NEW CREDIT

Getting a new car is very exciting. You get to pick the exact color you love, the body style, and the model. One thing you may not realize is that you may be getting a lower credit score along with that new car! Unless you already have high credit scores, a new car loan can lower your score. Having a car lease can affect your credit too. Remember creditors assume that when that lease ends, chances are good you will be looking for a new lease or a new car loan. If you are planning on purchasing or refinancing in the near future, it is a good idea to make sure that you either buy the car a minimum of six months before you apply for a loan, or just wait until after you've completed your mortgage loan.

Do not even think about getting new credit cards when you are considering buying or refinancing! However, if you don't have any credit, then the longer your credit history, the better your score will be, unless your credit history is filled with bad credit. If that's the case, then get a new credit card, even a secured credit card in order to show that you can handle the payments.

THE REST OF IT

Here is a common scenario: You are approached by your brother, sister, or friend who asks you to co-sign a loan so he or she can purchase a new car. This person's credit is bad; they don't make enough income or for some other reason, this person can't get a loan. My experience suggests that if a person cannot handle credit in order to get a car loan now, there's a good reason, and you should not be helping him or her. When you co-sign, that person's late payments become your late payments, their default is now yours, and that doesn't go away for seven years. Everyone wants to help people, okay, maybe that's just me, but in this case, your credit is something to be protected and preserved. It is hard enough to do this when you do have control over your payments and your credit. When you put yourself in a position where you have no control, it can impact your life.

You may not think you will consider buying a home in the next five years, but things can change. Suddenly, you may find yourself in my office having your credit pulled and finding out your brother, who promised that he would always pay the car loan that you cosigned for him on time, didn't. Maybe it's not his fault, maybe it is. Either way, your credit now stinks and you are going to pay for it in the cost of the loan, if you can even get a loan!

Parents often co-sign loans for their children, because they feel an obligation to help. If you feel this way no matter what I've just said, or you believe the scenario described above would never happen to you, at least let me tell you how to prevent late payments and collections. I've said this before, but it bears repeating! Have the person who is going to be making the payments send you their checks payable to the creditor. You mail the payments for them. This way you can be sure that they never miss a payment and the payments are made on time. This also gives you a way to show potential lenders that the payments are not yours. Make a photocopy of the checks every month. Then, mail in the payment.

If you are an authorized user on a credit card that means you are not responsible should the main card holder default on the credit card. However, any late payments that are made on that account and any monthly payments due as well are also yours, even if you are only an authorized user.

Hopefully, someone told you at some point in your life that credit is important and to take good care of it. When it comes to a mortgage loan, that couldn't be truer. Take care to ensure that your payments are always made on time, and resolve any credit issues immediately when you become aware of them. I find that many people tend to procrastinate, thinking that if they ignore it, it will eventually go away. Unfortunately, it never does. Items that negatively affect your credit will show up when you least want them to, especially when you are planning to buy a house.

I recently had a client that was preapproved by a major bank with just over a 620 credit score. When they reran her credit again after she had found a house and entered into escrow, she had a late payment on a local store credit card which dropped her score low enough to where she could not get a loan. Once she got that resolved (which held up escrow), she then had a late payment to Sears pop up as well. Now that payment to Sears was not late, but Sears reported it 30 days late regardless. Sears is not a credit card that is friendly to their credit card holders and they are difficult to work with when reporting your payments. They held up the client's loan to where she almost lost the house and only after the loan closed, did they correct their mistake...the client had NEVER been late!

One more item to be careful about today is disputing credit issues. Whether you are getting a conventional loan or an FHA loan, the guidelines for these loans do not allow for you to have a dispute on a credit card, collection or anything on your credit report. You will have to get that removed from your credit report before closing your loan. So be aware before disputing items if you are planning to buy or refinance in the near future.

If you are against having credit and don't want to get into trouble, it is important to understand that you need credit to get credit. Get a few credit cards with a low limit and don't charge much, but, you will need to charge something and pay it back. You need to show that you have a history of making payments in order to get a mortgage loan.

4

What to Expect
When Applying

So you've decided to buy a home. You've made
sure that your credit is good, you haven't
co-signed a loan for anyone, you have your funds to buy
the house, and you can't wait to start. What happens
next? What do you do? What is the process you should
follow so that nothing stops you from getting your dream
house? Here are some of the things you can expect to
happen during the loan application process.

The first thing you should expect after talking with
your loan officer is the process of getting your
documentation together. Your loan officer or mortgage
broker will tell you what documents you will need to
provide whether you are self employed, salaried, or an
hourly employee. Expect to gather tax returns, W-2's and
pay stubs covering at least your most recent month's
employment. You can also expect to be asked for bank
statements. Normally, this will include the last two
month's statements with all the pages.

I have many clients who do several things when sending me their bank statements. I inevitably have the client who wants to black out, cross out, or scratch out their bank account numbers or other information on the statements. WRONG!!! When someone is loaning you hundreds of thousands of dollars, they want to see proof of EVERYTHING! That means they need to verify that you have that account and the money is yours. It's like writing someone a check and crossing out your account number!

Another common mistake is to neglect to include the entire statement. When you have a bank statement that says page one of six, the lender will need all six pages. You may be thinking, "Well, page six is advertisements or blank." That doesn't matter. The lender will need to see all the pages the bank produced for your bank statement in order to ensure there is no missing information. If you know that you are going to be buying a home or refinancing in the next few months, plan on keeping all of your bank statements and pay stubs. Do not throw anything away!

There are many other pieces of documentation that your loan officer may request. The exact documents needed will depend on your specific loan scenario, as all loans are different. Keep in mind this next sentence as it is important. As soon as you tell people, which means your family and friends, that you are going to apply for a loan, they all will suddenly become experts. Now, I personally have no problem with your friends and family members giving you questions to ask your loan officer. They may see or think of things that you might otherwise forget to ask about. But, when they start telling you that they got this rate and this cost and why aren't you getting the same thing, it's because everyone's loan is unique. People have different credit scores, equity-to-value ratios, incomes, and so forth. The fact that your best friend got a better rate than you did doesn't necessarily mean anything. If you've picked the right loan officer, as we will discuss later, and you trust them, listen to what they have to say. If you find yourself not trusting your loan officer, then before you're in too far, find someone that you do trust. This is the biggest financial transaction of your life!

Based on your specific situation, you should receive loan disclosures in the mail (or via e-mail) that tell you specifically the terms of your loan, the costs involved, and all the information that has been included on your loan application. You should double check to make sure all the information on the application is correct. This way, if a number has been transposed on the application or other errors appear, they can be fixed *immediately*.

I once had a client who never checked the information on her loan disclosure forms, and her social security number was one digit off. She didn't check it, and the loan officer missed it. Even though the odds were that the lender would catch something like that, somehow the bank missed it too. Even when this client signed her loan documents certifying that her social security number was correct, she did not check the number. The loan got to the funding department where it was audited and the error was found. She lost out, because the loan could not close. At that stage, she had to have all of her loan documents redrawn and, in doing so, she lost a good interest rate because her rate lock had expired.

This sort of disaster can be avoided by simply verifying your information. People can always make mistakes, but it is your information that they have, and you need to verify it.

There are many disclosures, but some of the most important disclosure documents you will receive are included below.

The truth-in-lending statement, or TIL, is definitely one of the most confusing forms for both the person buying the house and many of the loan officers giving them out! This disclosure defines the terms and conditions of your mortgage and it can be the most alarming document, because it shows that if you keep your mortgage for the full thirty years, how much interest you will pay and the total amount you will pay all together over the entire term. It is usually three times as much as you borrowed, and when you are talking about hundreds of thousands of dollars, that's a big number! The part that is the most confusing for someone reading the TIL is the annual percentage rate (APR). (I told you that we love abbreviations!) Imagine that you've been told that your interest rate is, let's just say 4.875%. Now, you get your disclosures in the mail and you look them over. As you read the TIL document, you see a "rate" of 5.127%. You may say, "What? They lied to me. They told me that my rate was 4.875%, and now I see that it's really 5.127%." Then you get on the phone to call your loan officer on the carpet only to find that the "rate" is actually the APR. So, what exactly is the APR?

In simplified terms, it is taking the cost of the loan, including interest, points, and other costs, and annualizing it to an annual percentage rate. It is a way to compare rates and fees and to bring the rate to an even playing field. When you look in the paper or hear the ad on the radio talking about some amazing low rate, you may be able to get that rate, but how much do you have to pay for it? If the rate is 4.5%, your loan amount is $300,000, and you are paying 3 points (3% of the loan amount), your cost for points alone is $9,000! Is it worth it to lower your rate for that cost, and how long will it take you to make up that cost? Most of the time, it doesn't pay to do that but it sure sounds good! That's what the APR helps with. It lets you know what you are actually paying with everything included, so you can compare different rates and companies and costs.

APPRAISAL

The next thing you can expect is an appraisal. The lender will require that the value of the property be assessed by a certified appraiser. If you are purchasing a property, you probably will not be involved in the details of setting an appointment or meeting with the appraiser personally. If you are refinancing, you will be the one the appraiser will contact for an appointment. The process prior to May, 2009 was for your loan officer or loan broker to contact an appraiser, normally a professional who is in the area of your home, and hire them to appraise your property. Your loan officer would speak to the appraiser to make sure the actual market value of the property is in line with the amount being sought through your loan.

In the period since May, 2009 and as of this printing, a new set of rules has been put in place. This set of rules, called the Home Valuation Code of Conduct (HVCC) was put together by Andrew Cuomo, the Attorney General of New York and applied to the two government sponsored entities that purchase all conventional loans today—Fannie Mae and Freddie Mac. It is now also in effect for FHA loans as well. It no longer allows the broker to order an appraisal, instead, it must be ordered through the lender that your loan is being submitted to. The lender must order it through an appraisal management company (AMC) which uses a random process to choose the appraiser for your property. This is to ensure that the people involved in your loan transaction and who are getting compensated when your loan closes, are not putting undue influence on the appraiser. This is all for the best in theory. The main reason the HVCC was started was because some banks were using their own appraisal companies and threatening their appraisers if properties were not appraised at the values they needed. Now with HVCC, the banks *still* have their own AMCs and the main people being hurt are the appraisers and the consumers! Appraisers for conventional loans were normally paid about $350 per appraisal and received all of that money. Now, with the AMCs in the middle of the transaction, the cost of the appraisal is about $100 higher and the appraiser is making much less, as the AMC has to take its cut. As a result, we have found that the quality of appraisals has gone down. The appraiser is not necessarily in the same area as the property anymore. Indeed, they are often appraising properties as far as fifty miles away where they are simply not familiar with the market area. Knowing the market is a key to a good appraisal. For example, if you don't know that across a specific street is a different and more upscale area that has more value, a fact that you are not going to find on any map, you cannot value properties correctly. We are finding that is happening all the time now with appraisers who are not familiar with specific markets who are therefore giving poor and inaccurate appraisals. If the appraisal completed is not accurate or has flaws, fighting that appraisal is nearly impossible as the appraiser has no incentive to change it as they are paid so little to begin with. What do they care if there are inaccuracies or the value is not valid? They will still have business from the AMC and you are not their client.

This affects the customer more than anyone and costs them more money all the way around. In the past, I would have ordered your appraisal independently of the lender and then been able to shop for the best interest rate. I can no longer do that, because I have to order your appraisal through a specific lender, and once that's done, the appraisal is not transferrable to a different lender, unless it's an FHA loan. Instead, you will have to pay for a new appraisal through each lender. The same holds true if your loan is declined by one lender and we have to find another lender to close your loan. You will have to pay for a brand new appraisal. This is costing consumers hundreds of dollars more than under the previous system, and it is not benefiting anyone.

This process has truly destroyed people's livelihoods, cost money and time, and has accomplished little. The new Frank Dodd act allows broker's to order appraisals, but the people that govern Fannie and Freddie are still not allowing it. My personal opinion is that there is money to be made by the AMC's of which many are owned by the banks, so we won't see this change for quite some time...

Now let's move on and hope that your appraisal came in at a value you needed and your loan is moving forward. At this stage, you as the consumer are normally not aware of what's going on behind the scenes. So, here's a little snapshot for you.

UNDERWRITING

Your loan processor is taking all the information you have provided about your income and assets and all the documentation you have provided and is putting them together along with the title and escrow information to prepare a loan package that will be submitted to the lender and ultimately the underwriter. The underwriter is the person who checks all the documents to verify that all the information is true. He will verify your income, the money in your accounts, and all the information that has been provided and ensure that your application meets all the lender's guidelines. This is a huge job, as there are many guidelines (too many for me to cover in any one book). However, your loan officer needs to know many of these to be able to tell you which lender you should use for your loan if you are using a mortgage broker. At a bank, they cannot tell you that you cannot qualify for a loan as that would only be the underwriter's job. So, with a bank, you may not know if you qualify until the loan gets to the underwriter who will approve or decline your loan.

Once the underwriter does his job, he issues a "conditional approval." This document means that, based on the information the underwriter has, you now qualify for the loan, but there is more documentation that the lender will require before your loan is a done deal.

For example, if you had on your application that you receive overtime income of $1,000 a month, the underwriter will want verification from your employer that you've received that overtime for at least the past two years. Let's say you've actually received overtime pay for only one year and ten months, but you told your loan officer that it was two years because you rounded up. In such a case, you may no longer qualify for the loan. The underwriter will prepare a list of documents needed for verification in the form of a condition sheet and submit them to your loan officer. The conditions sheet will include items that are required prior to issuing your loan documents (PTD) and those that are required prior to funding your loan (PTF). In order to move forward with your loan, the processor will need to meet all of the PTD conditions to get you to the final stage of signing the legal documents for the loan. Throughout this stage, the loan processor will be working with you to put together any documents still required from you. The loan processor will also work with the title company, the escrow company, the realtors, and the lender in order to ensure all the conditions for closing and funding the loan are fulfilled.

Some people may think that they can go to any loan company, bank, or lender, because they are all alike. For example, they may assume that a 30-year, fixed-rate mortgage is the same regardless of where they apply for the loan. That is not true. While there is a basic loan that is available under Fannie Mae, Freddie Mac, or HUD (FHA loans), each lender can place restrictions or overlays on top of the basic requirements of those programs. For example, the Federal Housing Administration (FHA) does not have a minimum required credit score. However, most lenders today have a minimum of 620, and some have even raised that to 640. Although FHA will buy the loan with a lower score, the lender will not approve the loan. There are MANY overlays required by every lender and they differ among lenders. This is where engaging the help of a mortgage broker can make a huge difference, as brokers truly can shop among lenders to obtain not only the best interest rate, but also to see how individual lender guidelines can affect whether your loan will be approved or denied. If you apply at a bank and you don't meet its specific guidelines or overlays, your loan will be denied and you will have to start all over again with an entirely different loan officer.

The important thing to keep in mind when you are applying for a loan is that the underwriter is required to document everything. Therefore, your loan officer may well ask you to provide verifications and documents throughout the loan process. Most loan officers will try to get everything upfront, but sometimes they are asked for items that they didn't know the underwriter would request. Sometimes they might be hoping that the underwriter won't ask for certain documents, so they may not ask for them upfront. There is always a chance that one document may lead to questions or requests for other documents. I'm of the mind that it is best to keep it simple, but to understand what the underwriter will be asking for so you can anticipate the requirements in advance. Ultimately, what makes an underwriter happy is to have a complete file so that they won't have to ask for anything a second time.

In the months before purchasing a house, it is also important to avoid using cash for any major purchases or deposits. Cash is always a nice thing for most of us to receive, but for underwriting purposes, this is not the case. Cash is undocumented. Therefore, it is difficult to prove where it came from or how it was spent. So, please be careful not to deposit cash into your bank account as that deposit will need to be sourced and verified and that cash deposit may harm your ability to get the loan. Your down payment funds also need to be verified so if anyone owes you money, try to have them pay you back several months before you are getting a loan.

As the loan application process runs its course, your processor and loan officer will be working on your loan, even when you are busy with your life. If they are doing their jobs correctly, it should go smoothly for you! I recently had a client ask me how his purchase was going so smoothly, since he had heard that getting a mortgage was difficult. When you have the right people in place, it should go fairly smoothly. Inevitably, questions and problems will come up along the way, but a good loan officer will embrace the problem and come up with a solution.

5

Application Process

When I worked in a bank during that first thirteen years of my career, many clients would come in and ask me about loans. I would simply refer them to my loan specialist, who took care of them and helped them get their loans. At the time, I didn't know what a mortgage broker was or why anyone would want to use one as opposed to going directly into their bank for a loan. Now, of course, after being a mortgage broker for more than thirteen years, I have gained a different perspective on this question and want to offer both sides of the "banker or broker" debate.

BANKER, BROKER OR INTERNET?

When you go into a bank and ask for a loan, you will meet with a loan officer of that bank. Every lender and bank has their own set of particular guidelines, rates, costs, and fees. If you get a loan through a bank, you generally will have lower costs for originating the loan because there is no third party to pay. Typically, you won't have to pay for both underwriting costs and processing costs, because these steps are all completed in one place. The bank is both the processor and the underwriter. Some banks do charge an up-front application fee since they want to make sure that you don't start with them and then go somewhere else. Some of that cost may be credited to you at closing, but the remainder will be included on your settlement statement as just a fee. Whatever the bank's rates and fees are, that is what you will pay. You may not know whether these are good rates, because you can't compare them with those offered elsewhere.

You can go on the Internet to shop rates, but the reporting through the Web is not always accurate, and many times those lenders will post low rates to get you to pick up the phone to call them. Of course, once you do, you will often find that that attractive rate you saw is no longer available. Sometimes when banks get extremely busy, they will raise their rates to slow down business and get caught up with the volume. They assume that if you still want to get your loan with them, you will be willing to pay a higher price and that's fine with them. Currently, most major banks are taking 60 days to close a loan. You can get a longer time to "lock in" your interest rate by going with a bank, but it may take two months to complete your loan.

As a mortgage broker, I am decidedly biased on the question of why it is best to use a mortgage broker. I have some very valid reasons for this bias that I am going to share with you. When you apply for a loan through a broker, you complete only one application, submitting your income and assets and other documentation at one time and to one person. If there are any unforeseen issues with your loan application, the broker can submit your loan to a bank or lender that may be willing to work with whatever issue may have caused another bank or underwriter to decline your request for a loan. If you have such an issue and you request a loan through a bank or a direct lender, you may find your request does not meet the institution's guidelines. Then, you would have to start all over again with a completely different bank, lender, and loan officer. At each turn, you will have to start from scratch, telling your story, working through your issues, and beginning your loan application process all over again.

Dealing with a broker has benefits, even if you have the perfect loan application. A broker can shop for the best interest rates and costs, looking at many different banks or lenders to see what program will best meet your particular needs. Everyone has a story, even if he or she has great credit and great income. A broker can see which lender offers the best arrangement to fit your needs, as opposed to banks that usually take a one-size-fits-all approach. Keep in mind too that sometimes it is not the borrower that is an issue, but the property. Certain property types can cause a bank to decline you even when you have great credit, income and assets.

If you are computer savvy and feel you can figure this all out on your own using the Internet to see which lenders offer the best rates and terms, you can do that. However, you will not have the same relationship with someone you talk to only over the phone as opposed to an advocate you meet with in person. For example, the loan officer you call the first time may not be there the next time you call. What happens if you can't get a hold of the loan officer or they don't return your phone calls? What do you do then? You should be aware that when you work over the Internet, you just never know who is going to be helping you or what their experience is.

YOUR LOAN OFFICER

You've decided where you want to get your loan. Now you need to make sure that the loan officer you choose is one that you want to work with. Here are some things to consider before choosing this very important person.

Your loan officer, or mortgage broker, is the person who will explain the loan process to you, tell you how your loan works, and go over all the costs involved as well as the interest rate and so forth. In other words, this is your point person. You need someone who you feel comfortable with and who is competent. The question you really need to ask yourself is, "Do I trust this person to make sure that I am making the best financial decisions concerning the biggest transaction in my life?"

Your loan officer should be someone who is good at communicating with you. I once had a client complain to me that the loan officer she had worked with and who had handled all of her previous loans was not returning her calls. She had left many telephone messages and sent emails, but still hadn't heard back from him. My question to her was, "If he finally decided to call you back now, why would you WANT to have him arrange a loan for you?" If a loan officer or broker doesn't return your calls the first time or the second time, is this the person you want to trust to handle your loan? Is this a person you will feel comfortable spending time with and going over your financial and personal information? If so, when you get to the middle of the loan process and you still are not hearing back from this person, you might want to reconsider who you are working with. Your loan officer should be available either by phone or email when you need answers. The loan officer or broker's response may not be immediate, as he or she does have other clients and obligations, but they should be able to get back to you within a day, or if it is a critical situation, within a few hours.

Putting up with mediocrity from the person taking care of your biggest financial transaction is ludicrous. You should not tolerate it from the beginning. If your first impression of a loan officer or broker is not favorable, there is a reason. Always trust your instincts and don't go forward with anyone you don't trust no matter where the recommendation comes from.

It is important to ask how long the loan officer or broker has been in business and doing loans. I know of many people who are "loan officers" only because they were not making it doing retail sales or selling cars. Is that the expertise you are looking for? You should choose someone that either has experience in the loan business for at least three years or who has a great support team that has experience. Using your friend or relative is great, provided they have the knowledge needed to take good care of you and look out for your interests. If your relative or friend works with you on buying a home and they get it wrong, you could lose both the house and the friendship. One of the best ways to find a loan officer is to talk to your friends and relatives to get referrals on who they used.

People are always happy to refer people that were great. They will definitely be happy to tell you who NOT to use.

You also want to know who is on your loan officer or mortgage broker's team. It is important to know who will be processing your loan because that person is just as critical as the loan officer. They need to be experienced. Other members of the team are also important, as they are the ones putting your paperwork together and coordinating with all the people involved in your purchase or refinance. These people include, most importantly, your processor. If they give the lender incorrect documentation or don't give them the right documentation, it can mean the difference between getting approved or being denied. So make sure that when you are interviewing your loan officer, you know who will be working "behind the scenes" as well. The loan processor may very well be the person you end up communicating with during the loan application and closing process. Therefore, that person should be someone you can talk to as well.

WHAT YOU WILL NEED

Three years ago, you could easily get a loan with no income or asset documentation. At that time, stated income loans were all the rage. Under these loans, you could state the income you made. You didn't have to back it up with pay stubs, W-2s, or tax returns. The decision to lend was based on your credit score entirely. The better the score, the more likely you would not be asked to provide a lot of paperwork. In the most recent period, we have gone back to basics and everything is documented and sometimes, in my humble opinion, over documented. That being said, here's what you will likely need to provide your loan officer or mortgage broker when applying for a loan.

You will need a full month's worth of pay stubs. If you get paid twice a month, you'll need two pay stubs. If you get paid weekly, you'll need four. You'll also need your W-2s for the last two years and most likely, your federal income tax returns, or 1040s, for the last two years. People always want to give their state tax returns as well, but save yourself some time and a tree, they are never needed. I always try to keep the paper documentation to a minimum, and there are many times that I won't actually need your tax returns, but here is the problem that is arising now with not having them.

Let's say that you are a salaried employee working as a teacher at a school. You have your pay stubs and W-2s. I know that should be all that the lender needs to underwrite your loan. However, all the lenders now execute what is called a 4506T, which is a federal form that asks the IRS to give the lender a transcript of your tax return. If there is anything from your tax return that the lender doesn't know about that you didn't think was important to tell your loan officer, the bank will have that information from the IRS directly. Remember, the information filed with the IRS is what the lender will use. So, let's go back to your case. Say that you didn't think to tell your loan officer that you have a side business in addition to your regular job, and you receive income randomly throughout the year and you file a Schedule C, which is for self employment. This enables you to write off any losses you may have had through your side business. Remember, the fellow I told you about earlier who had a loss of $5,000 for the year on his tax return? It helped him to pay less tax overall, which was beneficial for his finances at the time, but then the lender had to deduct that $5,000 from his income. And, his loan officer never knew about it!

Knowledge in this business is critical. It is important to be sure your loan officer knows all about your finances in order to keep the application correct and to avoid any issues that may arise with the lender, including the possibility of having your loan declined, as in the case of the fellow who needed all of his income from teaching to qualify.

Here is another common example. Say you had a small rental property and you simply forgot about when you were talking with your loan officer, but you wrote it off on your tax return. If you don't remember to tell your loan officer, he or she won't know what documentation to get from you. So it's usually better to give your loan officer or mortgage broker copies of your tax returns up front so that there are no surprises during the loan process.

If you are purchasing a home, you will need to show that you have had the money needed to cover both your deposit and the closing costs in your bank account, stock account, or retirement account for at least sixty days. We call this sixty day period in advance, "seasoning of funds." Lenders want to know about any large deposits that have been made in the past sixty days and will ask you to document the source of those large deposits. Sometimes, the deposits do not even have to be that large, so be ready to document any deposits made outside of payroll deposits.

Lenders want to make sure that you haven't borrowed any of this money, as the funds need to come directly from you. In some cases, you can have gift funds. These are funds that are normally given to the home buyer by a relative without any obligation to pay it back to them. Those funds do not have to be seasoned, but the person who gave you the money will have to show that they had the funds in their bank account. The type of loan you are seeking will determine the amount of gift funds you can use toward your down payment and closing costs. For example, under the FHA rules, all the down payment and closing costs can be covered by a gift, and you don't have to have any of your own "seasoned" money. However, if you are seeking a conventional loan and you are putting down less than 20% of the purchase price, you will have to have at least 3% of the money needed for the down payment in your bank account. If you are putting down 20% of the purchase price, you may be able to use all gift funds.

One of the most common mistakes I come across with respect to funding the down payment and closing costs occurs when buyers purchasing a home give the wrong check for the deposit funds. What do I mean by the wrong check? For example, you cannot make a deposit using a credit card check, a check that represents a repayment of funds owed to you by another person, or by depositing cash into your bank and getting a check.

I realize this last alternative seems counterintuitive. Cash is always great to have, and in many cases it is the preferred choice. However, when you are seeking a loan, cash is the least desirable alternative to use, and it can actually create the most difficulty in getting a loan approval. You cannot document cash. Therefore, if you diligently save your money and leave it at home, under the mattress, in the cookie jar, or any of the other clichés, there is nothing to prove that you earned the money and it is yours. Lenders want to make sure that you have "skin in the game," and that the money you are putting down is really yours. This is why every lender requires proof and documentation about the source of funds for the down payment and closing costs.

The other pieces of information you will need to complete the loan application process are basic, like the addresses of your employers, the places you have lived for the past two years, and the financial accounts you hold. If you have any unusual circumstances related to your income or accounts or if there is anything you are not sure about, be sure to discuss this with your loan officer.

Sometimes it is the issues you think are the least important that turn out to be critical in terms of making the difference in getting a loan or being declined.

6

Different Types of Loans

FIXED RATE MORTGAGE

There are many different types of loans, terms, and programs to choose from, although there are considerably less now than there used to be. For example, you have the standard terms, which include a fixed interest rate on a mortgage set for a specific period, such as 30 years, 20 years, or 15 years. The longer the term of the loan, which is the amount of time you will have to repay the loan, the lower each monthly payment will be. The shorter the term of the loan, the higher the monthly payments will be. It is important to remember that monthly payments include both the principle based on the amount you are actually borrowing, and the interest you will be paying the bank to lend the money. Generally, loans with longer repayment terms carry higher interest rates, while short-term loans have lower interest rates. In today's market, the majority of people are getting these standard loans. They are often called fixed-rate mortgages, because the interest rate paid to the banks does not change over the term of the loan.

ADJUSTABLE RATE MORTGAGE (ARM)

There are adjustable rate mortgages (ARMs). These types of loans offer lower interest rates and are fixed for shorter periods of time, but the interest rates are adjustable. For example, you can have a loan with an interest rate of 3.5% that is fixed for a 5-year term, and then it will become an adjustable rate mortgage. In other words, subject to the market conditions, in five years your interest rate and monthly payments will change. How often an ARM's terms change and the parameters that allow it to change vary depending on the original loan terms set in the loan documents signed at closing. This is where it is critical to ask your loan officer or mortgage broker the right questions to ensure you understand what to expect over the course of your mortgage loan.

If you are not planning to stay in a property for more than the initial five-year period of an ARM mortgage, this type of loan may be right for you. These types of loans generally offer lower initial interest rates than standard fixed-rate mortgages. However, it is essential to understand what happens after the initial five-year period JUST IN CASE things change and you remain in the property. Will the interest rate go up to the maximum rate? How will the rate be calculated? How will changes in the interest rate work? These are questions you need to know. If your loan officer or mortgage broker responds to these questions with, "Don't worry about it, we'll talk about it in five years," run, don't walk away!

There are two reasons some loan officers or brokers will not want to give you a straight answer to those questions. First of all, the loan officer or broker may have no idea how your loan works, so they may not be able to explain it to you. Second, they are not offering good terms and they don't want you to know it. While the adjustable rate mortgage can be a great choice under the right circumstances, it is important to discuss all your options with a loan officer or mortgage broker who is knowledgeable about your situation and all the loan instruments available.

If you are putting down at least 20% of the purchase price of your new home, or have at least 20% equity in your home when you refinance, chances are good you will be seeking a conventional loan. This means you will not have a loan that is guaranteed by the government, as in the case of an FHA loan or a VA loan. It also means that you won't have any mortgage insurance.

MORTGAGE INSURANCE

What is mortgage insurance? Some people refer to it as PMI, which simply stands for private mortgage insurance. It is insurance that you pay to a mortgage insurance (MI) company for the lender's benefit, not your benefit. If you default on your loan, the insurance company will reimburse the lender for some of the loss. As you might realize, the MI companies have taken a beating given the unprecedented number of foreclosures that have been taking place since 2007, so their guidelines for lending have become much more difficult than they used to be. Their guidelines are on top of the ones already in place for your loan, so you must meet both set of guidelines if you are putting down less than 20%.

Because of the sharp rise in foreclosures, getting a conventional loan in today's market is much more difficult than it has been in the past unless you are putting down 20% of the purchase price. The MI companies have made their lending guidelines very strict and limiting with the amount of coverage they offer lenders. In fact, many of them will not underwrite loans at all in Arizona, California, Florida, and Nevada, due to the many foreclosures and property devaluations that have taken place in those particularly hard hit states. They are starting to loosen up, but not completely. The loan of choice and of necessity at this time is the FHA loan due to the credit and underwriting guidelines.

FHA stands for Federal Housing Authority. This is an agency governed by the U.S. Department of Housing and Urban Development (HUD). The most popular misconception about FHA loans is that they are only for first-time buyers. That is not true. In fact, whether you have purchased a home before does not come into play with an FHA loan as long as you didn't default on that loan. What does matter is that you plan to use your new home as your primary residence. FHA lends only on owner-occupied properties, not second homes or investment properties. These loans are meant to support home ownership in this country, and the mortgage insurance that you pay goes to HUD.

You will be required to pay mortgage insurance whether you put down 3.5% of the purchase price, which is the minimum down payment at this time, or more than 20%. FHA loans have different standards in underwriting than conventional loans. Although the most popular difference is the low down payment required, there are many other differences that make FHA loans attractive.

First, you can have someone that is not living with you be a cosigner on your loan in order to help you qualify. For example, if you are making enough money to afford your new home, but part of your income is from overtime, that overtime may not be used to qualify you for the loan. Therefore, based on your regular income alone you can't buy a house. You remember that your parents mentioned at one time (when they weren't thinking straight!) that they would help you if you wanted to buy a house. So, you give them a call and find that they would be happy to cosign with you and help you to qualify. They then become what we call "non-occupying" co borrowers. Under this rule, you may buy your house. However, your parents will be responsible if you don't pay the mortgage, even though they will not be living in the property.

Second, unlike the rules about conventional loans that we talked about earlier, you can get a gift for the full amount of the down payment and still qualify for an FHA loan. With conventional financing, you can use all gift funds only if you put down 20% or more of the full purchase price, but if you are putting down less than that, you have to have at least 3% of the down payment of your own money.

Third, the interest rates on FHA loans are typically about the same as conventional loans, but you will pay both an upfront mortgage insurance premium as well as monthly insurance premiums. This increases the amount of your monthly payments. FHA has increased their monthly mortgage premiums over the past few years. Since the time I have been doing loans, the monthly MI premium was .55%. Currently it is 1.15% which is more than double what it was before. This has made FHA loans more expensive to borrowers.

FIXED VS. ARM

There has been much written about ARM loans. These loans can be good for the right reason and the right client. An ARM loan has a fixed rate for a specified period, such as one year, three years, five years, seven years, or ten years. After that period, the rate becomes adjustable for the remaining term of the loan which can vary. But, the standard term of a mortgage loan is thirty years. One reason to get an adjustable rate mortgage is that these loans usually offer lower interest rates than a standard 30-year, fixed-rate mortgage, at least during the initial period of the loan. This makes this type of loan attractive as a way to get a lower monthly payment for the first few years that you own your new home.

If you don't plan to keep the house long term, then an adjustable rate mortgage may be right for you. Of course, plans sometimes change, right? So, what happens seven years later when you are still in the house you bought with the intention of staying for only five years?

Here are some keys to guide you through the things to look for in deciding whether an ARM is the right loan for you.

Everyone looks at just the initial interest rate on the adjustable, but the key element is the margin on the loan. What is a margin? The margin is basically the profit margin for the lender. Essentially, this is what is added on to a base interest rate, which can be the one-year Treasury bill, the six-month LIBOR, or whichever index the lender decides to use as a base interest rate for your loan. The margin is a big piece of what your actual interest rate will be, so ask your loan officer about this. Of course, when it comes to margins, lower is better. When the interest rate on your loan is adjusted, it will most likely be close to whatever the market rate is at that time. A typical margin is about 2.75%. Let's look at an example.

I had a client that recently asked me what was going to happen with her adjustable rate mortgage. The time for the interest rate adjustment was approaching, and she was freaking out! She had a 5.5% interest rate and was deathly afraid that it was going to go up over 7%. But, here's the reality of her situation. The basis, or index used to set her interest rate was the six-month LIBOR, which is a very common index to use. The LIBOR was at 1.36% and her margin was 2.75%, which is a decent margin to have. When you add the index plus the margin (1.36 + 2.75) you get a new interest rate of... drum roll please ... 4.11%! So now you are wondering whether her interest rate really adjusted from 5.5% to 4.11%. The answer is "yes," owing to this adjustment, her interest rate and monthly payments actually went down. This is happening with most of the people that have ARMs right now. The indexes are very low, so the interest rates on many loans are adjusting to less than the original rate. Many people have chosen to remain in their adjustable rate mortgage and ride it out through the financial crisis. You can estimate how your interest rates will be adjusted under your ARM by looking up the index and margin used. This information is included in your mortgage note.

JUMBO LOANS

If you are purchasing a property that is above the conforming loan limit, you will have to get a loan with a lender that specializes in Jumbo loans. Conventional loans are currently at a maximum loan amount of $625,500.00, although that is the maximum and it may be lower depending on your county limits which are all different. FHA loans are still guaranteed at this printing to be at a maximum of $729,250.00, again based on your county limits. Any loan amount that meet these conventional or FHA limits is considered a conforming jumbo and although it is conforming, there are still different guidelines and rates associated with those loan amounts. The conforming loan limit at this time is $417,000.00. There are many private lenders that will offer loans above the conforming limits, but they are more restrictive and may require larger down payments.

The last type of financing is called "hard money." These lenders have access to private money, but they normally have much higher interest rates and require much more money down in light of the risk they will be taking. Your interest rate can be anywhere from 8% to 16%. The cost of the loan will also be much more expensive than a conventional loan, so think very carefully before getting a hard-money loan to ensure the benefits outweigh the risks.

Figuring out the right loan term and type is something that you should be able to discuss with your loan officer. Everyone has different needs, and all of your needs should be taken into account when completing your loan.

7

Interest Rates

If I'm at a party, a luncheon, or dinner and the topic of what I do comes up, the first question I inevitably hear is, "So, what are the rates today?" As much as I would love to just spout numbers, my telling you the current interest rates without having any information about your particular situation is like a doctor offering a diagnosis on why you're not feeling well just by looking at you. The interest rates applied to individual mortgage loans are determined by many different factors. Therefore, giving you a standard, pat answer to the above question doesn't do anyone any good.

What are the factors that determine your interest rate and how can you find ways to get the best rate for your own situation? Read on.

One of the biggest mysteries associated with interest rates are points. I know, "What is a point?" you ask. A point is a percentage of your loan amount. If you have a loan of $300,000, one point would be $3,000. This is part of the cost of a loan and a point can be charged for many different reasons. The main reason to pay a point upfront is to buy down to a better interest rate over the life of the loan. All mortgages come at a cost, so the lower the interest rate, the higher the cost will likely be in terms of points. Of course, at higher interest rates, you may have no points.

How do you know if it makes sense to pay points and buy down your rate? Well, if you have an interest rate of 5% and you pay one point to lower your rate to 4.75%, you will save on your monthly payments. For example, let's use that same $300,000 loan. One point is $3,000.00 up front, but your monthly payment goes down by $45.51 a month. If you divide the $45.51 into the cost of the point, $3,000.00, you get $65.92. Thus, it will take 5.5 years to make up the cost needed to reduce your rate. Is that worth it? Well, I have my own rule of thumb that I use with my clients. This rule of thumb is, if it takes less than three years to make up the cost, pay the point and lower your rate. If it takes longer than that, it really depends on your financial picture and how long you think you will stay in the house. Many people end up moving sooner than they originally planned or they end up refinancing. Either way it would destroy the reason for paying the points.

Based on my experience originating loans over the past eleven years, it seems a point normally reduces the interest rate by only a .25%. In most cases, paying the point upfront doesn't usually make sense. However, there was a six to nine month period in 2009 when a point bought nearly a .50% reduction in the interest rate. In that situation, paying the point up front did make sense.

Often, when you see advertisements for really low interest rates, you find when you talk to a loan officer that the low rate isn't really offered. Did you ever wonder why not? It's because the lender is basing the advertised rate on charging points, and the cost to get that "too good to be true" rate is much more than would make sense for most borrowers. This is one of the reasons you always need to find out the whole story about a loan, not just the part that sounds really good. Sometimes people call points by other names, such as origination fees or discount fees, but they are still points.

If you are refinancing your property, any closing costs for the loan, including any points that you do choose to pay can be added to your loan balance and financed over the life of the loan. Many people choose this option, since it means they don't have to take money from their bank account to refinance their mortgages. However, when you are purchasing a home, you don't have that option. The only way that you would not have to pay all the closing costs along with the down payment is if the seller agrees as part of your negotiation to pay for your closing costs. That is something you can discuss with your realtor when making offers on property. This is a standard part of the negotiations between you and the seller. Otherwise, you will have to come up with the money for both your down payment and your closing costs. It is important to know up front what your closing costs will be and be prepared for them, as your closing costs can sometimes be as much as the minimum down payment.

Aside from reducing the interest rate on a loan, another reason you might be charged points could relate to the type of property you are buying. Some lenders associate points with some kinds of properties, such as condominiums, townhouses or investment properties. If you don't have at least 75% equity in these property types, the lender will likely charge you some points when you are purchasing or refinancing. There are almost always points associated with loans on investment properties, regardless of the size of the down payment or the amount of equity held in the property. For an investment property, the points can range up to 3 points charged by the lender. You can either pay the points upfront or you can offset some of the costs by raising your interest rate. This again is something you should discuss with your loan officer to determine what is the best option for you.

Some of the other reasons you may be charged points would depend on the loan-to-value ratio, which is the amount of equity held in the property, and your credit score. Generally, if you don't have a FICO score of at least 740 and you have a loan-to-value ratio of 60% or more, you may be charged some points. If you are taking cash out of the property when refinancing, you will again see some points based on the loan-to-value ratio and your credit score. These are all things you should discuss in detail with your loan officer.

Another important question to ask is how your loan officer gets paid. Every interest rate has a cost or a rebate, and the interest rate determines the profit or cost. When the interest rate is higher, part of that profit is given to the broker or the bank. When a loan is a "no points" loan, it is because the broker has been paid the points by the lender, which is usually set as a percentage of the loan amount. Brokers are paid by points whether the lender pays it through the interest rebate or the borrower pays it as an origination point. A broker can determine how many points that they make, and the lender will pay the broker based on that rate. The reason rates differ from place to place and broker to broker is that the brokers can choose how many points they will be paid for each loan. As a mortgage broker, I have to disclose how much I make on each of the loans I close, but a bank, even though it may make the same amount I do, does not have to disclose what it makes on a given loan.

Interest rates on mortgages are set by the mortgage bond market. Just like the stock market, they go up and down every day, which is why rates change every day. Just because the bond market moves doesn't mean that everyone prices their loans the same way. Every bank and lender has a secondary marketing department that determines what price it will pay or charge for every rate available. That is one advantage of working with a mortgage broker; their ability to shop for lenders with more aggressive rates. Once a bank sets its rate, that is the only rate a loan officer working for the bank can offer you.

When I worked for Cal Fed Bank as the branch manager, there was a time when it was really busy and the volume of requests for loans was tremendous. Loans were taking sixty to ninety days to close and everyone was getting frustrated. What do you think the bank did? Did they hire more people or find a way to speed up the process? No. They raised their interest rates above the average to slow down the requests for new loans coming in. I have found through the years that when lenders get busy, they raise their rates. They assume that people who want to give them their business will pay the higher rate. If the lender makes more profit, the extra effort is worth it. The converse is also true. If lenders are very slow and need to bring in more volume, they will lower their rates and cut their profits.

Knowing where to look for the best interest rates, the right programs, and the guidelines that will get your loan approved is a mortgage broker's priority and main area of expertise. Banks simply cannot do these things for you. If you fit into their guidelines and are willing to pay their rates, a bank may be the place for you. I would not only shop for rates and fees, but also for a loan officer who is going to work for you and for your benefit. What would I look for in a loan officer? I would definitely want someone who would go beyond merely quoting me a rate. I would want someone I could work with who would take into account my complete situation and financial picture and not just be trying to make a quick sale that they may, or may not, be able to close. I would also be aware again that the bank's loan officer is not allowed to tell you that you would not be approved when you are submitting your loan application. They can tell you that you can apply and then the bank underwriter will determine if your loan can be approved. I have helped many clients that were preapproved by a major bank only to be declined right before they were supposed to close the loan. What did these clients do? They came to me where I could identify the issue that they had and send their loan to a lender that I knew would approve their loan and save them from falling out of escrow. I had one client where the bank that had declined him was the bank that my lender ended up selling his loan to. It's better to know up front what can and can't be done when buying a home and a broker can tell you that up front and save you time and money.

Your time is valuable and the services of a loan officer or mortgage broker are invaluable.

8

What are My Costs?

Whether you are purchasing or refinancing, when you have a loan there are more "moving parts" than you could imagine. As with most things, there is a cost to everything. Understanding what those costs are, what you can negotiate, and what you can't, takes a lot of frustration out of the loan process. You should have a good idea of the costs involved and who they are being paid to from the start, when you are deciding who you want to work with. Some of the costs you will be paying are going to be unknown at the beginning. For example, if you are purchasing, your loan officer won't know who will be taking care of your escrow and title, and those are key components of your loan and your costs. What is given to a client at the beginning of the loan application process is called a good faith estimate or "GFE." It is just that: an estimate of all of your costs and fees. Of course, every effort is made to get an estimate that is as accurate as possible. There are some general formulas that are used to calculate the escrow and title fees, but that doesn't mean that the escrow company is going to use that same formula. Sometimes the fees can be much more or much less! Having said that, the loan officer or mortgage broker should be exact about his or her own fees. She may not know yet which lender your loan will be going to (as a broker), so she may not know the fees to charge for a particular lender. Lender fees can range from $695 to $1200. In actuality, getting the numbers exact at the very beginning of the loan process is nearly impossible for a purchase.

As of January 2010, HUD has mandated a new Good Faith Estimate (GFE) for costs associated with a loan and it has many different components from the past. An estimate given within three days of an application must have all of the correct fees and if there are discrepancies in certain fee areas, the loan officer is responsible to pay the difference. For example, if I take an application and I pick a lender that has a great rate for my borrower and their lender fee is $800 and I put that on the GFE, then that is the lender fee I have to charge to my borrower at the end of the loan transaction. However, if before I submit the loan to this lender, XYZ lender has a much better rate for my client and I now submit the loan to them, but their lender fee is $850, I would have to pay the difference of $50. The same would apply for an appraisal, which is paid to the appraiser. If I am told the cost is $400 and that is on the GFE, but the appraiser has to reinspect the property and charges an additional $100, I would have to pay the $100 if I didn't disclose that fee upfront.

What this means is that now, since I don't always know as a broker which lender I will submit any given loan to, I will quote the highest lender fee to my borrower so that I will not have to be responsible to pay the difference. That doesn't mean that they will be charged that high fee, just that it will cover me no matter which lender I choose that has the best rate for my client.

Here are two more changes that will have a huge impact on your estimate and costs.

On a purchase transaction, the buyer typically will pay for a title policy called a lender's title policy. The seller of the property pays for their title policy called an owner's policy. Even though the buyer will not be paying for the owner's policy in addition to their lender's policy, the GFE must now have that amount on the estimate. It will also list the cost of transfer taxes which is also typically the seller's responsibility, but this must be listed under the buyers cost or the loan officer has to pay for that cost, which is not even an actual cost to the buyer!!! Confused yet? Welcome to the new world of lending where the government imposes rulings that make no sense in the real world of mortgage lending.

The other change is, the rebate that the broker is getting based on the interest rate that was chosen, (a no points loan where the lender pays the points due to the loan officer), is now credited to the borrower. This means that all brokered loans will show origination points in order to pay the broker, offset by the lender crediting the buyer the rebate from the rate. Sometimes the credit from the rebate is higher than the points charged which makes the cost of your loan less as well. This is even more complicated than I am showing here, but understand that the estimate that you will receive is no longer giving you the correct estimate on what funds you would have to bring in to escrow when you close your loan. Why? Because most loan officers will over budgeting their estimate to ensure that they don't have to pay any differences and they will be including both title insurance and transfer taxes that you don't have to pay at closing.

Trusting your loan officer will be a huge part of making sure that the people that are overinflating their numbers are truly not taking those funds in the end. HUD began this with good intentions. This new estimate was meant to get rid of the bad players in the marketplace; the ones that promised low fees and costs and then didn't deliver at closing. However, the way that this has played out in the real world is not as expected, and has created more customer confusion as many of the fee's are now lumped together and not broken down. You no longer know what you are being charged from each party in the transaction. As always with any regulated industry, it is what we have to deal with and hopefully explaining its components will help you understand the new process.

Here's a breakdown of the people you pay when you purchase or refinance.

Lender – The lender fees can vary depending on whether you are going to a bank directly or going through a mortgage broker. If you are going to a bank, you will still pay for processing and underwriting, but normally the fees overall will be slightly lower than when you go through a broker. This is because the bank will put those two fees together, and you are only paying the bank's cost. When you use a broker, they will place your loan with a wholesale lender or a bank, but you have their lender fees in addition to what the broker charges for processing. The normal fees you can expect to see would be for processing, credit reports, the appraisal, and underwriting. You will also sometimes see fees that the lender charges, such as an administration fee, document preparation fee, funding fee, tax service fee, and flood certification. Some people call everything that is charged a junk fee, but many are real costs that are passed down to you, the borrower. In this respect, they are not "junk," but some, such as processing and underwriting fees, have profit built in. Everyone has a staff that processes, underwrites, and draws loan documents and funds, so they are paying their staff with those fees. Junk or not, some cannot be quantified, like a credit report or an appraisal. Labor costs are more difficult to quantify, so you will see a wide range of fees that vary among different banks, lenders, and brokers. No two companies' costs are going to be exactly the same.

Escrow – The escrow company is the neutral party that deals with all the money involved in the transaction between the buyer and seller in a purchase, and between the borrower and the lender in a refinance. The escrow company is there to make sure that the financial terms of the purchase are carried out as set forth in the contract. This includes the purchase price, the division of costs between the buyers and sellers, and so forth. In some states, this escrow function may be met by a real estate settlement firm or an attorney. In any event, the company that handles the escrow will normally charge a settlement fee to both the buyer and the seller. Its job is to coordinate with the title insurance company, handle the loan documents with the lender, and arrange the signing of the documents. At the closing, this company makes sure that everyone is paid in accordance with the purchase contract and the lender's instructions for the loan. They may also charge what's called a loan tie in fee, a wire fee, a messenger fee, an email doc fee, and other fees. Again, these fees will vary among escrow companies. Some escrow companies seem to charge a lot more than others. When you purchase a property, the seller normally picks the escrow company, so you have no choice on which company you use. Then, you are stuck with whatever fees the company charges. If you can find out which company will handle the closing soon after you enter into escrow, you can get a list of the company's fees and see if there is anything they can do to reduce the cost, but it's like walking into a store and asking if they can reduce the prices because you don't like them. Can they? Possibly, but they have set their fees for a reason and may not be willing to lower them because you aren't happy. The difference here is that you don't have to buy in any given store and can walk away. With an escrow company, you usually don't have that same luxury and have to work with them and buy their "products."

Title – Title insurance companies are involved in every purchase transaction, even if you buy a home for cash. They are also involved in every refinance. Title insurance companies are responsible for making sure that as a buyer, you will have a clean title from the seller before you purchase the property. Let's say that you decide to buy a home and the title insurance company finds that there is a lien against the property owner. Perhaps, the owner didn't even know about it. That lien would have to be paid off in order for the seller to pass on a clear title to you. Otherwise, the chain of title could become a legal mess over time, or over the course of several transactions. If the title insurance company didn't find the lien, but it showed up at a later date after you purchased the property, the title insurance would protect you.

Similarly, in the case of a refinance, a title search is conducted to ensure that there aren't any liens against you or the property that the lender doesn't know about. If you had a tax lien, judgment, mechanics lien, or similar encumbrance, the title insurance company, closing agent, or attorney will provide the lender a preliminary title report that shows what taxes are owed against the property, who owns the property, what liens against the property have been recorded, and so forth. In some cases, even when buyers have paid off a loan, a previous lender may not have recorded a "release of lien" or reconveyance to show that it no longer has an interest in the property. Again, that is something that the closing agent or title insurance company will take care of on your behalf.

I had an unusual situation where the client on a refinance had a mortgage he had been paying for eight years but the preliminary title report didn't show the lien against the property that had to be paid off. In his case, the lender had never recorded the deed of trust against the property. His original loan was still paid off with his refinance, because we knew he had the loan, but you have to wonder if he sold the house what would have happened with the lien that was never recorded. There are many legal situations that can come up with a property title. Now you know why you must pay the title insurance company each and every time.

When you are purchasing a home, you don't pay as much for the title report as the seller pays since your policy is a lender's policy, not the owner's policy. For a refinance, you pay more, because you are required to have an owner's policy.

The cost of title insurance is based on the loan amount both on a purchase or a refinance. There is also a sub-escrow fee that is charged unless the title and escrow company are the same company. The only way to describe this fee is that it is charged to coordinate between title and escrow. There will also be a wiring fee, since closings normally entail wiring money from the lender to the escrow company, which then pays the seller and all the other parties involved in order to settle your escrow account.

Broker – Fees from the broker can vary just as any other vendors' fees. There are a few that you can expect most of the time. There will almost always be a processing fee. The processor is very important in a loan transaction. In this respect, the processor is sometimes even more critical to your loan than your loan officer. That's because the loan processor is the person who puts all the information that you've given the loan officer together and makes sure that it is presented to the lender clearly and in accordance with the lenders' guidelines. If a processor doesn't do their job correctly, it can make or break your loan. Once the loan is underwritten, the lender will give a conditional approval, or an approval that says once they have any items that they require, they will fund your loan. Some of those conditions must be met prior to getting the loan documents and some are required prior to closing and funding your loan. The goal of the processor is to get your loan documents and meet all the conditions required for funding once the loan documents have been signed.

Another fee a broker would have is for your credit reports and the property appraisal, but the broker only collects these fees from you and passes them on to the credit report company and the appraiser. Typically, the broker does not get any of these funds. Some brokers will charge an administrative fee, which is for the cost of their staffs, photocopying, and the cost of your loan. Some charge a warehouse fee, which is to pay for their bank line if they fund their own loans as a mortgage banker. Some brokers charge an application fee and other fees that cover their costs. Overall, the total will vary from broker to broker. Again, some people call any and all of these "junk," but many of the fees charged by a company are set to cover their costs and also make a profit.

Nobody works for free and quite honestly, they shouldn't have to. A loan is a complicated and important financial transaction, and the broker keeps all the parts running smoothly for you. At least that's what they should be doing. Yes, there are people that overcharge for their services. But that's what shopping is all about. You should shop for any service that you want to use and look at the whole picture, not just the fees. It's about trust, cost, professionalism, and whether you want to do business with a certain person. If you feel that your loan officer or broker has your best interest at heart and is competent and knowledgeable, you may want to go with them, even if that option is more expensive than the company that doesn't return your calls or forces you to chase down answers to your questions.

There are so many moving parts to a loan transaction. If you are purchasing a home, there are more people involved than you may realize. All of these people have one goal in mind, and that's to close your loan. Some work together well and some are more difficult to work with, but in the end, closing is the name of the game. Nobody gets paid if your loan doesn't close. How many companies can spend a month or more working on a project and never get paid if it isn't completed? Most will get paid something along the way, but in the loan business, the parties involved only get paid when your loan closes.

9

The Final Stage

Okay, so you have met your loan officer, gotten preapproved, shopped for a home, put in an offer, and started your loan. You've put all the paperwork together, signed everything you thought you had to, and gotten a loan approval. Now, you want to know what's going to happen, and when you are going to close.

So much will have happened from the time you gave your paperwork to your loan officer and they gave it to the loan processor. The processor has taken care of coordinating with the escrow company and the title insurance company to get the documentation needed, ordered the property appraisal, and put your loan together in order to meet the lender's guidelines and get your loan approved.

Once there is a complete package of all the documentation required, the file is submitted to the lender or the bank, where it is now placed in a stack of other loans just like yours waiting to be underwritten.

The underwriter then reviews and underwrites the loan. This person examines and verifies all the details of your file and issues a conditional approval, which is sent back to the processor. The processor then requests any additional information or documentation that is needed from you, the escrow company, the title company, and many times from the appraiser or other parties. The loan processor puts all of these items together and submits them back to the lender where they sit and wait for the underwriter to review them again. After this final review, you are good to go forward in most cases. Sometimes the underwriter will ask for more conditions or need more information. This process can be repeated over and over again, depending on how thorough the original submission of documents was and how picky the underwriter is. Just like anything else in life, it can depend on the person that you get, and you can get an underwriter who seems to want a LOT of things or one who seems to be happy with what you sent them. Unfortunately, it's all the luck of the draw.

Once the underwriter has signed off on all the conditions that are needed prior to issuing the final loan documents, the request for loan documents is submitted to the lender and you wait for the lender to prepare your loan documents. The amount of time this takes varies among lenders. Some lenders allow the broker to draw up the final loan documents on their systems, but most do not. If you are a broker that is a correspondent with the lenders, you can draw up your own documents, which is usually quicker than waiting for the lender. Either way, the final loan documents are normally sent directly to the escrow company, where arrangements are made for you to sign them. **These are official, legal documents, and it is imperative that they are correct in setting forth the terms of your loan agreement.** The interest rate, the repayment period, and the overall cost should be what you have agreed with the lender or broker. There should never be any surprises at this final stage of the game!

In the past, shady lenders and brokers often would take advantage of people by quoting a set of terms to get business, and then change those terms at the end. It often seemed that these people offered a deal that was "too good to be true," and many times it was, in fact, not true! This is called a bait and switch, when a lender quotes an interest rate or cost that cannot be done just to get you to come to them for a loan.

I have never engaged in such practices. Telling people what I can do, and what they can expect, is part of my business and my personality, and I can't imagine doing it any other way. However, I have heard plenty of stories from my clients who have been taken advantage of in the past. Here are a few of the most common tales:

I had a client that was told there were no prepayment penalties on his loan. When he went to sign the loan documents, it stated that there was a prepayment penalty. He called the broker, and the broker said there had been a mistake that he would fix, but that my client needed to sign the documents presented. Of course, my client believed this broker and signed the documents. Sure enough, he later found that he had a prepayment penalty. The loan documents you sign are official and binding. In other words, after these documents are recorded, you cannot change key points, such as the repayment term, the interest rate, or any penalties. Therefore, do not sign your final loan documents if you are not sure you are getting what you think you are getting! Too many people didn't understand the type of loans they were signing when the ARM and negative amortization loans (also called option arms) were predominant. They either didn't understand or didn't want to understand. Either way, it was a mistake to sign the final documents.

I would advise you to have your loan officer send you the estimated HUD settlement statement before the closing. This statement shows all of the costs and charges for all of the parties involved, just like the good faith estimate that you got from your loan officer at the beginning of the process. This pre-closing HUD settlement statement should be completely accurate. Your loan officer should review it with you to make sure that it's accurate.

Many times, particularly if you are using an escrow company or a closing agent, the person handling the signing may not be familiar with loans and is just there to witness your signature and notarize all of the documents. If you are not sure while you are signing your loan what something means or if it's different than you expected, ask the person handling the closing to explain it. If he or she doesn't know the answer to your question, call your loan officer or broker immediately and ask him or her to clarify the matter. In some states like California, it may be possible to change some items, like deciding to have your taxes and insurance impounded after the signing is completed or the escrow company removing an incorrect fee as long as the lender hasn't mandated that fee. In other states, this cannot be done without arranging for a completely new signing. In any event, it is not possible to change other key terms, such as the interest rate to be charged, the amount of the loan, or the period for repayment. Therefore, you should not sign the closing documents unless or until these items are correct, and don't listen to anybody who tells you differently!

What happens after the loan documents are signed may vary among different lenders, brokers and banks. Typically, the loan documents are returned to the lender where a funder reviews the documents for accuracy as well as any other outstanding items that the lender required prior to funding your loan. This reviewer will also verify your employment on the day of funding to ensure that you are still employed before they fund your loan. If you lost your job that morning or the day before, the lender will not fund your loan. Obviously, lenders cannot verify employment for self-employed borrowers. They will also have gotten the results from a form called a 4506T that goes to the IRS where they verify that the information you provided them matches the information on your tax returns filed with the government. If there is any discrepancy, you will have to show why and provide proof of the income reported. Most of the time this form is completed before getting your loan documents, but occasionally it is done before funding your loan.

Sometimes after loan documents are signed and you feel like you are done, you find you are not quite finished with the transaction. There may be a missing signature in the stack of documents or the lender may have forgotten to include a document you are required to sign, or they may want an updated paystub. Sometimes, there may be an item they requested before, but they cannot find it or didn't receive it. This is the final stage, and before they actually fund your loan, the lender has to be sure they have all of the documentation necessary to close their file.

If you get a last minute phone call from your loan officer, or the escrow company, it is because they are trying to get your loan funded and completely closed. In this situation, time is of the essence, since they normally have only a very short period in which to get this information to the funder. Lenders generally will stop funding loans at a set time every day. Whatever last minute requests might entail, simply go with it, relax, and work with whoever calls to get whatever documentation is needed. Remember the parties involved are trying to close your loan! Normally escrow will have their own specific set of conditions to gather for the funder and the broker may as well, so you may get calls from each of them for different items needed.

Once your loan has been fully funded and the money has been wired to the title insurance company, the property deed and the deed of trust are recorded. In some counties, the court clerk can record a deed on the same day the loan is funded. In other counties, such as Los Angeles County in California, the deed of trust cannot be recorded until the day after the loan has been funded. If you are buying a home, this means the house is not yours officially until the deed is recorded. If you are refinancing, it means that your old loan is not paid off until the deed is recorded; therefore, you are overlapping one day's interest on two loans, your old loan and your new loan. Many lenders don't like to fund loans on Fridays if the County can't record the same day, especially on a refinance, because you will be paying interest on both loans over the weekend. This can often amount to hundreds of dollars.

Once the new deed is recorded, if you just closed on a purchase, you will be getting the keys from your realtor and focusing on moving in and all of the chaos and joy that that entails. If you refinanced, hopefully you will have accomplished what you wanted and now can relax!

The loan process is one that changes on a regular basis and no two clients are alike. At the same time, no two lenders are alike, and no two loans are alike. This keeps all of us on our toes. Remember, as you go through this process your loan officer is going through it with you every step of the way, and making sure that you are getting the best loan with the best possible terms.

I hope that the information I've given you in this book will help the process go much smoother. You have done the research and now know what you need to do long before you apply for a loan. This will help your loan officer to do their best on your behalf, and make your loan much less stressful. When you are buying a home, you should be focusing on the move itself, arranging the packing, the movers, and so forth. My goal is to help ensure that your loan is the one thing you should not have to worry about. Knowing what to expect can save you time, money, and frustration.

Use a FREE QR Reader App on your SmartPhone to scan and enjoy!

 Scan the QR code to get immediate access to a mortgage calculator to help you see what your payment might be and for other stress free tips and offers!

CPSIA information can be obtained at www.ICGtesting.com
Printed in the USA
BVOW04s1224230114

342806BV00004B/255/P